MYSTERIES UNCOVERED

Mysterious Worlds

by Craig Boutland

Gareth Stevens PUBLISHING

Published in 2027 by
Gareth Stevens Publishing
2544 Clinton St.
Buffalo, NY 14224

For Brown Bear Books Ltd:
Children's Publisher: Anne O'Daly
Design Manager: Keith Davis
Picture Manager: Sophie Mortimer

Picture Credits
Front Cover: Shutterstock: Framalicious.
Interior: iStock: 19, 24; Shutterstock: 20, 22, Carlos Aranguiz 6, Daily Traveler 11, Deniz Esin 5, Oscar Espinosa 14, Framalicious 28, Zack Frank 18, Hecke61 13, Gert Hochmuth 21, Nataliya Hora 17, Xuan Huongho 10r, Lano Lan 10l, Alberto Loyo 7, Magic East 12, Maxx-Studio 8, MisterStock 15, Mozgova 9, Vadim Petrakov 16, Dmitry Pichugin 29, rb3legs 27, Robert Harding Video 26, Alexandre ROSA 23, thipjang 4, Waj 1, 25.
All other artwork and Photography Brown Bear Books and Shutterstock

Words in bold appear in the glossary on page 30.

Cataloging-in-Publication Data
Names: Boutland, Craig.
Title: Mysterious worlds / Craig Boutland.
Description: Buffalo, NY : Gareth Stevens Publishing, 2027. |
Series: Mysteries uncovered | Includes glossary and index.
Identifiers: ISBN 9781482479003 (pbk.) | ISBN 9781482479010 (library bound) |
ISBN 9781482479027 (ebook)
Subjects: LCSH: Earth sciences--Miscellanea--Juvenile literature. |
Geographical myths--Juvenile literature. | Ghost towns--Juvenile literature
Classification: LCC GR940.B68 2027 | DDC 550--dc23

Printed in the United States.

CPSIA compliance information: Batch #CS27GS: For further information contact Gareth Stevens at 1-800-542-2595.

Contents

INTRODUCTION

On September 12, 1940, a French teenager named Marcel Ravidat led some friends into a cave near their village. According to a local story, lost treasure was buried there. Instead of treasure, the boys found paintings of animals on the cave walls. They told their teacher, who called in an expert. The paintings were found to be 17,000 years old.

The caves have more than 600 paintings, which mainly show large animals including horses and deer.

Monasteries in Metéora, Greece, were built high on rocky outcrops.

Hidden Places

The story of the Lascaux Caves is an example of rediscovering something hidden. This book will show you other hidden places. There are tunnels that allowed soldiers to hide from enemy forces and abandoned towns that were once full of people.

Some places became hidden because they were abandoned and forgotten. Others were hidden deliberately. Some were visible but impossible to reach. These hidden worlds may give us a better understanding of the visible world around us.

Giant STATUES

Easter Island is one of the most remote places on Earth. It is 1,290 miles (2,075 km) from its nearest inhabited neighbor. In 1722, Dutch explorer Jacob Roggeveen became the first European to visit.

Roggeveen saw hundreds of giant stone heads. The statues were up to 30 feet (9 m) tall and weighed up to 80 tons (72 tonnes). They had been carved from volcanic rock by the Rapa Nui people who lived on the island. The islanders called these statues moai. They used them to honor their **ancestors**. Between about 1250 and 1500 CE, the Easter Islanders carved more than 1,000 of these statues.

The statues have large heads. Their faces have deep-set eyes and a long nose.

Some moai were set up in rows on stone platforms.

Walking Statues

Once the statues were carved, they were moved to special platforms called ahu. The Rapa Nui likely moved the heavy statues using ropes. Experts believe they "walked" the statues by rocking them from side to side. Some statues may also have been dragged on wooden sleds or rollers. Moving them required careful planning, strength, and great teamwork.

MYSTERY UNCOVERED

Civilization Collapse

Some historians think the moai led to the collapse of the Easter Island civilization. Carving the statues took a lot of time. Without being looked after, the land could not support all the people. Eventually many people left the island.

The Center of EARTH

Many ancient cultures believed Earth was hollow. The Greeks thought the dead lived in underground caverns. In Navajo mythology, the first people are said to have risen from inner worlds within Earth. It wasn't until the 19th century that scientists confirmed the center of Earth is solid.

The center of Earth is made of iron and nickel. The outer core is liquid, and the inner core is solid.

Early scientists suggested Earth was a hollow shell. But in the 19th century scientists showed that could not be true. If Earth were hollow, it would have less mass, and **gravity** would be weaker than it is. Today, we know that Earth has a rocky core at its center. Earth's surface is a series of plates that float on layers of **molten** rock.

MYSTERY UNCOVERED

Through a Volcano

In 1864, the French novelist Jules Verne wrote *A Journey to the Center of the Earth*. The novel describes an expedition into an extinct volcano in Iceland. The volcano leads to a world with oceans and storms, but no inhabitants.

Holes at the Poles

Scientific proof didn't end the idea that Earth is hollow. Early in the 19th century, John Cleves Symmes argued that there were holes at the poles that led to worlds hidden inside. Even in the 20th century, some people still argued that the human race had emerged from inside Earth, through a large hole at the north pole.

Symmes tried to raise money to visit the North Pole to prove his theory.

Rebel TUNNELS

In the 1950s, rebels against French rule in Vietnam began to dig a system of tunnels beneath Saigon (now called Ho Chi Minh City). The rebels hid in the tunnels when they began to fight the French.

By the 1960s, the rebels were known as the Viet Cong. They began fighting U.S. troops based in Vietnam. The tunnel system was 75 miles (121 km) long. It was entered by secret trapdoors. Many of the tunnels were too small for people to stand up in.

A tunnel (above) and a secret entrance (left).

The catacombs of Paris were built in old tunnels.

MYSTERY UNCOVERED

The Catacombs
Beneath Paris, France, a mile (1.7 km) of tunnels was used in the 19th century to bury the dead. The tunnels are called **catacombs** and hold thousands of skulls and other bones. They were first dug to get stone to build the city.

Difficult Conditions

The network connected kitchens, command centers, and **dormitories**. The Viet Cong stayed in the tunnels in the day and came out at night to launch attacks. Conditions were hard. The tunnels were full of snakes, rats, and scorpions. Most of the rebels got sick.

The tunnels gave the Viet Cong an advantage in the Vietnam War. The U.S. Army bombed the area, but couldn't destroy the tunnels. Today, the underground network is a popular tourist attraction.

China's Lost PYRAMIDS

China's "lost pyramids" were never really lost. Archaeologists knew about them. These massive flat-topped mounds near the city of Xi'an were built as tombs for ancient Chinese emperors.

Exploring the "pyramids" later led to the discovery of 38 burial mounds. The largest belonged to the first emperor of China, Qin Shi Huangdi. Ancient accounts said that the emperor's tomb was huge. It had taken more than 700,000 people to build it between 246 and 208 BCE. Inside, the chamber was modeled on the emperor's capital city, Xianyang.

Qin Shi Huangdi's tomb is buried under a forested hill.

Imperial Tomb

The emperor was buried with many servants. They were sealed alive in the tomb, in order to serve their master in the afterlife.

The emperor's tomb has not been opened. But in 1974, farmers dug up old remains nearby. In one of the mounds, archaeologists found an army of **terracotta** warriors standing guard over the tomb. There were more than 8,000 life-sized soldiers, together with chariots and horses.

MYSTERY UNCOVERED

Rivers of Mercury

Qin Shi Huangdi's tomb has still not been opened. Experts want to wait until they have developed techniques to preserve its contents. Also, ancient accounts say that the tomb included rivers of mercury, which is highly poisonous.

The lifesize clay soldiers were intended to protect the emperor after his death.

Hidden in CAVES

In 1819, British army officers were hunting tigers in the jungles of central India. They found the entrance to a cave carved into a cliff and decided to explore. Inside the caves, they were amazed to find remarkable religious sculptures and paintings.

In all, the builders had carved 30 caves into a rock face hidden in a ravine near the village of Ajanta. From the statues and paintings, it was clear that the **monuments** had been dedicated to the Buddha, the founder of Buddhism. We now know that the caves had been built between 230 BCE and 500 CE. They were part of a Buddhist monastery. One of the caves featured a large hall for worship and a number of cells for the monks to sleep in.

This statue of the Buddha is inside one of the caves.

Abandoned and Overgrown

After the monastery had been used for over 700 years, it was abandoned. New caves were left unfinished. The monks and the builders left, and the jungle grew back over the entrances. When it was found again in the 19th century, everyone had forgotten it ever existed. Nobody knows why the caves were suddenly abandoned. It may be that Buddhism became less popular than India's other major religion, Hinduism.

MYSTERY UNCOVERED

Carved in Rock

Temples were carved into rock across India. It may have been easier than digging out rocks to make a stone building. The builders often carved the caves as if they were built of wood. For example, they carved roof beams that were not actually necessary in caves.

The Ajanta caves had been overgrown by jungle.

Gateway to the AFTERLIFE

On the Yucatán Peninsula of southern Mexico are a series of flooded caverns. For the Maya people who lived in the area, the caverns were a source of water but they were also sacred places.

The caverns are known as cenotes. The Maya believed they were gateways to the **afterlife**, the home of the dead. The **sinkholes** were created when limestone was eroded by the underground water that lies beneath much of the Yucatán Peninsula.

The cenotes were a key source of drinking water for the Maya.

Limestone **stalactites** hang above a cenote.

Some of the cenotes are like open pools. Others are dark wells that are lit only by a small opening overhead.

Sacred Sacrifice

To the ancient Maya, the cenotes were sacred. They threw valuable objects into the water. The Sacred Cenote is a pool outside the city of Chichén Itzá. The Maya thought it was the home of the rain god Chaac. At the bottom of the pool, archaeologists have found weapons, tools, jewels, and carvings that were thrown in as **sacrifices** to the gods.

MYSTERY UNCOVERED

Human Sacrifice

Among other objects that have been found in the cenotes are human skeletons. It seems that the Maya sacrificed humans to their gods. They probably threw the victims in alive and left them to drown or starve in the caves.

Ancient Cliff DWELLINGS

In the southwestern United States, ancient buildings sit beneath cliff overhangs high above the ground. The cliffs offered protection from harsh weather. They also protected from enemies and wild animals.

The cliff-dwellers who built these hidden communities are known as the Ancestral Puebloans. These Native Peoples lived in the Southwest between about 1190 and 1260 CE. At sites like Canyon de Chelly in Arizona and Mesa Verde in Colorado, they built homes from sandstone. The homes were joined to one another, with doorways in the roofs. The cities were built for defense. The only way in was by ladders, which could be pulled up as protection against attack.

The cliff dwellings at Canyon de Chelly in Arizona provided natural protection.

A Place for Rituals

The monuments feature circular, half-buried pits. These are known as kivas. The pits were used for religious **rituals**, but no one is quite sure about their purpose. What little we know about the peoples today comes from pottery they made or drawings they left on the walls. In the 13th century, the people left their homes and migrated south and west, where their descendants still live.

MYSTERY UNCOVERED

Climate Change

Why were the cliff dwellings abandoned? Some experts believe that the climate changed in the 13th century. The Ancestral Puebloan lands became drier, and crops failed. No defenses could protect the people from the environmental disaster.

Mesa Verde is home to dwellings and circular kivas.

GHOST TOWNS

Not all hidden worlds are from ancient cultures. There are more recent settlements around the world that were flourishing places but fell into decline. Today, the people who lived there are virtually forgotten.

An old yard in Bodie is home to a rusting car.

The ruins of a town called Bodie lie high in the hills east of the Sierra Nevada, in California. They stand alone along a dirt trail, miles from any highway. Bodie boomed in 1876, when gold was found nearby. Up to 7,000 people arrived in a few years, and the town had 2,000 buildings. But the gold soon began to run out.

Buildings survive from Bodie's Wild West history.

Mines were opened to dig for other **minerals**, but they closed one by one. By 1940, only 90 people still lived in Bodie. The buildings were rotting and abandoned. Streets that had once been full of miners and gunfighters were empty apart from tourists.

Modern Ghost Towns

An even more recent ghost town is Picher, Oklahoma. In 1996, scientists found that lead mines had contaminated the town's water supply. The government bought the houses and moved everyone out.

MYSTERY UNCOVERED

Ghost Cities

Some ghost towns are abandoned before they are even occupied. From 2000, the Chinese built new cities they hoped would attract many people. Economic changes mean the cities are still waiting for residents who may never come.

Building UNDERGROUND

Coober Pedy is a mining town that lies in one of the hottest parts of the Australian desert. If you were driving through, you would see a small collection of huts. But below ground, nearly 2,000 residents live in special "dugouts."

Most of the people who live in Coober Pedy are miners. The town was founded early in the 20th century, when opals were discovered there. Opals are valuable gemstones that are often used in jewelry.

Salt miners carved out chapels deep in the Wieliczka mine in Poland.

Conditions were hard for the miners who came to dig the opal. Daytime temperatures in the summer often reached as high as 104°F (40°C). The miners dug homes into the hillsides around the town. They built stores, bars, and churches under the ground. The earth keeps the rooms at a constant temperature, no matter how hot or cold it is above the ground.

MYSTERY UNCOVERED

Salt Carving

Salt has been dug at the Wieliczka mine in Poland since the 13th century. Miners began to carve religious statues deep in the mine. Eventually, they created dozens of statues, three chapels, and a whole cathedral underground.

Underground Walkways

Underground buildings are used elsewhere too. PATH is a network of walkways and pedestrian tunnels under Toronto, Canada. The tunnels connect more than 70 buildings and protect residents from freezing winter temperatures and heavy snowfall.

At Coober Pedy, most of the town's life goes on underground.

Cave DWELLINGS

Cappadocia in central Türkiye is hot and dry. Its harsh, rocky environment has very little wood to build with. Instead, the people who lived there carved homes into the remarkable rock formations.

The first underground buildings were made in the eighth century BCE. Early Christians later built churches there. The religion was illegal in the Roman Empire. The Romans often killed or arrested Christians. The Christians used tunnels to escape **persecution**.

The "fairy chimneys" are made of soft rock called tuff.

The cave homes were important centers for early Christianity.

Underground Cities

The underground city of Kaymakli was linked by more than 100 tunnels. Derinkuyu had enough tunnels to shelter 20,000 people and their animals. The best-known cave buildings are near Göreme. The soft rocks have been eroded into columns called "fairy chimneys." They were easy to hollow into homes and churches. Early Christians carved small cells for themselves where they could meditate without distraction.

MYSTERY UNCOVERED

Troglodytes

People who live in caves are known as troglodytes. Thousands of modern-day troglodytes live in caves around the world, including in Tunisia and China. Near Granada in Spain, old cave dwellings have been renovated with electricity and running water.

CAMELOT

King Arthur was a legendary British king. He ruled his kingdom from a castle at Camelot. Arthur gathered the Knights of the Round Table. They went on quests throughout the country, fighting for justice.

Many historians doubt that King Arthur existed, but other people think the stories were real. They try to find the location of Camelot. An English writer Sir Thomas Malory wrote about King Arthur in the 15th century. Malory said Camelot was the castle at Winchester, in southern England. Winchester had a round table, like in the story. But the Winchester table was made in the 14th century, 800 years after Arthur was supposed to have lived.

The ruins of Tintagel cling to a tiny island just off the coast.

The hill fort at Cadbury was dug into the top of the hill.

MYSTERY UNCOVERED

Arthur's Stone?
Arthur was said to have been born at Tintagel Castle. The castle's ruins lie off the coast of Cornwall. In 1998, a stone from the sixth century was found there. It was carved with the name "Artognou." Some people thought this is linked to Arthur, but experts say there isn't enough proof.

Cadbury Castle

Another suggested site of Camelot is Cadbury Castle. This hill fort stands near the Cam River in west England. Many nearby place names include the **syllable** "cam." Could this have been Camelot? Archaeologists dug at the site in the 1960s. They found a large fortification—but no evidence to link it to King Arthur and his famous knights.

Mountain MONASTERIES

Buddhism began in India in the sixth century BCE. By 1200 CE it was almost unknown there. Despite its decline in its homeland, the faith survived in a few remote monasteries.

These monasteries were founded high in the Himalaya Mountains. Few outsiders visited them. When the Islamic religion pushed Buddhism out of much of India, it did not reach mountain kingdoms such as Tibet.

Paro Taktsang, also called the Tiger's Nest monastery, was built on the site of a sacred cave.

The monasteries stood high on mountain ledges or perched on the edges of ravines. The Tiger's Nest monastery in the Himalayan kingdom of Bhutan stands 2,300 feet (700 m) up a cliff face above the valley.

Saving the Faith

Safe in the monasteries, monks studied the teachings of the Buddha. They wrote down copies of Buddhists' holy **scriptures** and made sure that the faith survived. Eventually their efforts helped lead to a revival of Buddhism across the rest of India.

MYSTERY UNCOVERED

Monks of Metéora
Monasteries have often been built in high places for defense. At Metéora in Greece, six monasteries were built on top of natural pillars of rock. All the building materials had to be lifted to the top. The monks were raised up in baskets.

The monasteries of the Himalayas were built to be easily defended.

GLOSSARY

afterlife In some religions, the place where people go after death

ancestors The people from whom living people are descended

archaeologists People who investigate traces of the past

catacombs Underground cemeteries located in tunnels

dormitories Rooms where a number of people sleep

dugouts Shelters that are dug into the ground

gravity A force that attracts objects toward one another

minerals Useful substances dug out of the ground by mining

molten Melted, used to describe something that is usually solid

monastery A place for monks to live and worship in that is cut off from the everyday world

monuments Things made in remembrance of the past

outcrops Rock formations that stick out of the ground

persecution The ill-treatment of people based on race or religion

rituals Religious ceremonies that follow a fixed order of events

sacrifices Valuable things given as offerings to the gods

scriptures The holy books on which a religion is based

sinkholes Holes worn in the ground that let water flow into underground passages

stalactites Rock formations that hang from cave ceilings and are formed from minerals in dripping water

syllable A single unit of sounds that makes up a word

terracotta A type of pottery made from hardened clay

FIND OUT MORE

Books

Bradshaw, Eleanor. *20 Things You Didn't Know About Easter Island* (Did You Know? Wonders of the World). Powerkids Press, 2024.

Sonneborn, Scott. *The Paris Catacombs: Empire of the Dead.* Capstone, 2025.

Spilsbury, Louise. *Earth's Most Mysterious Places* (History Raiders). Crabtree Publishing, 2021.

Websites

Cave Dwellings
A look at some modern-day cave communities and underground towns
www.nationalgeographic.com/culture/article/cave-dwellers-human-adaptation

China's Pyramids
Encyclopedia Britannica article about the tomb of the first emperor of China
kids.britannica.com/students/article/Qin-tomb/609602

Ghost Towns
Descriptions of six ghost towns around the world, including Bodie
www.bbc.co.uk/bitesize/articles/z2rmg2p

INDEX